In Praise of the Author's Work

"Thurman's inspirational journey traces from the depths of trauma and addiction to his monumental casting out of the '*Dragon*s' that held him back for so long. His creative redemption narrative explores, through verse, prose narrative, allegory, and visual arts, his excruciating yet necessary confrontation of his '*Dragon*s' (such as negative self-talk, externalized shame, and the false need to blame others). This allowed him to make room for growth in spirituality and self-affirmation of worth. Dancing in the Light offers hope to people who wish to make positive changes in their lives. This edifying example of spiritual rebirth and recovery highlights how we all have the potential to win against our personal '*Dragons*' and reclaim the beauty of the present. It is a beautiful book."

Heather R. Hayes, M.Ed., LPC
Heather R. Hayes & Associates INC., *Founder and CEO*

"The longest, hardest walk I've ever had to make was from the parking lot to the front door entering the treatment center. I had come to the end of life as I knew it. Sad and broken, I was convinced I would never be happy or whole again. Thurman smiled – and proved me wrong. It started with a kind understanding ear and progressed to fearless transparency from his journey to helping me to find mine. In time, joy returned to me. Thurman showed me that my past doesn't define me but will always serve as the line of demarcation that we all must cross at some point if we want to be kind, dependable people. I will always credit him for helping to save my life."

Edwin McCain
Singer-Songwriter, Musical Artist

In Praise of the Author's Work

"As I read this remarkable book of abuse from an alcoholic father and the recovery of the child whose defenses were the 'Dragons of Dysfunction and Pain', I recall two of the author's quotes: 'It is better to be hurt than to be scared' and 'Healing doesn't require the absence of discomfort, only the freedom from victimization.' The book revisits these statements and reveals the hopeful messages of addressing your '*Dragon*s' of self-talk, pain, and despair and changing the 'Dragons' of self-destruction into "dancing in the light". Thurman Strother has written a very powerfully painful – but also very healing – story that anyone who has experienced any type of trauma should read. Dancing in the Light is simply the best recovery book that I have ever read."

Dr. Merrill Norton Pharm.D.,D.Ph.,CMAC
University of Georgia, *Clinical Associate Professor Emeritus*

"I have known Thurman for over thirty years. He is a therapist extraordinaire and understands the recovery process of addiction / mental health like no other. I have always admired his heartfelt ability to inspire those that struggle with shame and hopelessness."

Michel A. Sucher, M.D, DFASAM
Sucher Medical Management, Ltd., *President*

"I had the great honor of working and learning so much from Thurman Strother about the disease of Addiction. This wonderful book illustrates the beauty of getting your life back after it had been hijacked for so long. Thurman told the wonderful and clever parable of *Encountering a Dragon* to literally thousands of patients over the years, which comes with added sound effects when delivered live. This story has helped turn on the light for so many health professionals."

Bill Braun, MD
Board Certified Addiction Medicine

In Praise of the Author's Work

"My journey with Thurman Strother for nearly four decades has always reinforced my belief that recovery and freedom exist beyond the pain of addictions. Now, Thurman has blessed readers with his personal and professional journey in the recovery process that illustrates the concept of emerging from darkness to light." Thurman Strother's book, *Retired Dragon Fighter - Dancing in the Light*, and the parable, *Encountering a Dragon*, both beautifully describe a recovery journey that embodies the paradox of 'we surrender to win.' Also, he happens to be the kindest 'Retired Dragon Fighter' you will ever meet."

Jim Daniel, NCACII, CCS, MAC

Retired Dragon Fighter
SERIES

Thurman Strother

Copyright © 2022 Thurman Strother
Softcover ISBN: 979-8-218-04610-1

All rights reserved. No part of this book may be reproduced or transmitted in any form or by any means, electronic or mechanical, including photocopying, recording or by any information storage and retrieval system, without permission in writing from the copyright owner. For information on distribution rights, royalties, derivative works or licensing opportunities on behalf of this content or work, please contact the publisher at the address below.

Cover Art: Thurman Strother
Editors: Alle Byeseda & Lucy Lee
Layout: Alle Byeseda

Although the author has made every effort to ensure that the information and advice in this book were correct and accurate at press time, the author does not assume and hereby disclaims any liability to any party for any loss, damage, or disruption caused by acting upon the information in this book or by errors or omissions, whether such errors or omissions result from negligence, accident, or any other cause.

To Mom and Dad.
LOVE
689

CONTENTS

FOREWORD	xi
FROM THE AUTHOR	xv
PROLOGUE	xix

Part 1

Birth of a Dragon	3
Dragon's Roar	7
Safety in Silence	9

Part 2

Weapons of Mass Destruction	15
Lost in a Masquerade	17
Over the Edge	19

Part 3

Running to Escape	25
Search for Sanity	27

Part 4

Movement Towards Truth 33
Force Against Force 35
Recognizing the Enemy 39
Here Comes the Sun 41

Part 5

Healing in God's Will 49
Giving to Receive 55
Treasures of the Heart 57

Epilogue 61

ENCOUNTERING A DRAGON

Prologue 67
A Parable 73
Questions for Discussion 83

About the Authors 89

FOREWORD

A young tree grows better when it's planted in an area with older trees. The roots of the young tree are able to follow the pathways created by former trees. Over time, the roots of many trees graft to one another, creating an intricate, independent foundation. In this way, stronger trees share resources with weaker ones so that; as a whole, the forest becomes healthier and stronger.

Like the root system of a thriving forest, the roots extended by Thurman have affected thousands of individuals seeking positive life change. Thurman's legacy is difficult to put into words; it is best depicted in terms of an experience.

Thurman's goal is always about the solution, seeking clarity by the route of keeping it as simple as possible. You know he cares – you can feel it.

Thurman hears you and speaks right to the spark that is inside all of us. He loves easily; he fights for all patients to have a voice. He will walk with you through the darkest time in your life with a light of guidance that you can trust.

When I reflect on the time I spent working with Thurman, I remember that he wouldn't let people take notes during educational groups. He

Foreword

would ask the group to just listen, be open-minded, and find their own words.

Thurman always has been humbled by the courage that it takes for someone coming into treatment to share openly and ask for help and direction. He honors the trust and willingness that it takes when a patient shares their truth by asking for help to embrace life as a part of something greater than themselves. He always would describe this sharing exchange as a profoundly spiritual experience.

When Thurman asked me if I would write the forward for this book, I was; of course; honored – but equally shocked. I wasn't shocked that he asked me, I was shocked that he finally wrote a book! People have asked for his words in writing for a long time.

I, for one, know that I'm just happy that it has finally happened.

Jennifer Angier, MS
Meadows Behavioral Healthcare
Vice President of Addiction Services

FROM THE AUTHOR

I was honored to work in the field of Mental Health/Addiction Recovery for over forty-five years. In that time, I worked with many amazing clinicians and patients, learning daily from our shared experiences; I am forever grateful for all those teachers.

Some of the most profound lessons I ever received were given to me by the thousands of men and women that filled the rooms and chairs of recovery programs; the courageous, strong warriors that shared their truth in quest of a purposeful life of freedom. It was those experiences of trust and caring that created the bond of mutual spiritual exchange that continues to be my mission.

I retired in 2016 because of health issues. It wasn't long before I missed the wonderful exchange of the spirit that gave my purpose a home. When I realized that purpose doesn't have locational boundaries, I found a renewed sense of purpose in writing this book.

In *Retired Dragon Fighter - Dancing in the Light*, I share my journey as evidence that grace not only resides in joyful experiences of life but is present in our most challenging times as well.

Courage and strength exist in embracing all emotions, emphasizing the distinct difference between emotional truth and the punishing self-talk that is disguised as emotional truth. Maintaining hope in darkness is a courageously spiritual act of faith. Living life as life presents itself is the foundation of spiritual existence.

The included parable, *Encountering a Dragon*, is co-authored with Alle Byeseda. Alle happens to be my daughter and, obviously, a significant player in my spiritual journey. Her talent and creativity add color and insights to the overall meaning and purpose of this book. Its purpose primarily is to serve as an educational tool and teaching opportunity for individuals and families. Our hope is for readers to recognize the *Dragon*s in their lives for what they really are. The goal is to take the insights and suggested skills provided to vacate your mind's dialogue of any *Dragon*s, while relying on guidance that is based in truth, hope, and faith.

DEFINITIONS OF A DRAGON

Oxford Languages, s.v. "dragon (n.)."

: a mythical monster like a giant reptile. In European tradition the dragon is typically fire-breathing and tends to symbolize chaos or evil…

My "*dragon* (n.)."

: a response to trauma that manifests in a collection of powerful distortions

: a force that resists any attempt to reach the truth.

Other Names: *Self- talk, Self-will, Storyteller, Slick*

DRAGON
FRIEND OR FOE?

Within everyone's journey through life, many actions of trauma can occur. In those cases our defenses kick in, rushing to protect us from the intensity of the distress. Sometimes, positive, productive strengths and skills can courageously overpower or change the course of these challenges. But sometimes, those same defensive coping mechanisms have a different outcome. The initial defensive response is based in self-centered fear that can use variations of coping to lessen or conceal the threatening force. Any traumatic occurrence can prompt such an action. This defensive response is not a weakness or flaw, but is simply a reflex response to trauma.

Unfortunately, the flight of escape (coping) can manifest in a collection of powerful distortions of self thoughts and harmful behaviors. If these distorted thoughts and harmful behaviors remain intact, they will block you from a reality that demands responsible action. In other words, that which once protected us, turns against us. It becomes; a force that will resist any attempt to reach the truth. Any attempt to defeat a *Dragon* becomes a counter-force against you.

The cause of the trauma is NOT a *Dragon*! What happened to you is not a *Dragon*! A *Dragon* is the distorted, dysfunctional self-talk that guards against the emotional truth of the trauma.

It is necessary to distinguish between emotional truths that need to be expressed and experienced, and *Dragons*, or non-productive beliefs and judgments, that block your freedom and separate you from God's grace.

To become a warrior against the forces of a *Dragon* does not require a weapon of force. In competing against a *Dragon*, hope is the sword and faith is the shield that drives the courage and strength to resist the battle all together. This is where you will find freedom through acceptance. This is how you can become a warrior against the forces of a *Dragon*.

You see, the real victory is to achieve freedom from the corruption of the distorted beliefs of the *Dragon's* roar. The victory is in moving from darkness to light, sadness to happiness, being alone to being connected with others, and hopelessness to faith.

My sincere desire is that this book prompts an experience, giving you helpful insight to avoid self harming efforts that happen when trying to defeat a *Dragon*.

This book will offer you safe and successful approaches to healing from the wrath of traumatic, unresolved emotional conflicts. The parable, *Encountering a Dragon*, is appropriate for all ages. The book, *Retired Dragon Fighter - Dancing in the Light*, is suggested for adult readers.

PROLOGUE

Dancing in the Light

Living free from the grip of self-centered will,
allows you to embrace the grace that surrounds you.
Connection with that grace is our purest action of spirituality.
Spirituality can't be defined in theory or belief; spirituality is a beautiful movement of living exchanges that embraces God's grace.
God fills the space that connects us, which finds the path of profound purpose.
This union creates the rhythm that drives a dancing of the spirit.
Dance is when rhythm, melody, tone, and harmony are aligned,
awakening expression through movement of your body and spirit.
When dancing is necklaced with the grace that surrounds us,
a beautiful symphony of spiritual presence is composed.
This dancing of the human spirit reaches that area that we really can't explain.
It's the place where the music of the heart can be heard,
where our soul breathes, where faith is realized, not spoken.
To sway in rhythm with glorious flair, enjoying the presence of united love.
Smiling, "Dancing in the Light" of beauty and grace as your soul is kissed from above.
Sometimes music requires volume to reach the soul.
Sometimes the soul requires silence to feel the music.
Although self is only one, we are a precious one;
humbly gifted to be part of a greater whole.
Together blessed with the intention of shared love;
sharing purpose in beauty of the enlightenment of our soul.
~ Dancing again ~

PART 1

Chapter One

Birth of a Dragon
Lost Boy

My brother, Shelby, turned out the light, the comic book finally tossed to the floor. It won't be long before I can do what I need to do.

My father is not home and that means my mother is still awake… worried, sad, and probably angry.

I have been pretending to be asleep for the last thirty minutes. I am good at doing that when I need to be. I listen to the sound of my brother traveling into a deeper sleep, hoping that I won't be too late to get to my spot on the steps.

Ready to make my move, I slowly slip from my bed, creeping silently to leave the bedroom. I know the pathway easily, even in the dark, because I have made this trip many times. I can slightly see the outline of the bathroom door, indicating that I am yards from my destination.

The Steps…

Those three steps are where I can hide.

From there I can retreat to my bedroom if needed, or rush to the living room if required. From there I can hear and see any activity from the front door to the living room.

My mom; sitting in the living room; can't see me, as she sits nervously waiting for my father to come home. If I lean forward, I can see her fidgety feet as she sits in her flowery colored chair. From the flickering light and the little muffled sound, I can tell the TV is on. I don't think she is watching the TV… only using it to break the silence.

I remain very quiet to avoid being detected. It will upset my mother if she sees that I am still awake; if she knew that I was worrying about her.

My mom's mission is to see if my father gets home safely. My mission is to see if my mom will be safe when he gets home.

I am never sure what I can do to help my mom, but I feel like I need to try. I've got my baseball bat with me just in case my father comes home in a bad way and ever hurts her.

He better not hurt her!

When my mom cries, I want to hit and hurt something… but I can't.

I sometimes pray that my father never comes home again. When my father doesn't drink alcohol, the house is a much safer place. I can't let any of my friends come over to the house. I can't predict what things will be like. I can't spend the night at my friends house because I need to be here if my mom needs me.

One time, my father's car totally burned in the middle of our front yard. It was crazy and embarrassing . Many times when he didn't come home, we found him asleep in his car where he had passed out – never making it in the house.

When my father is raging and starts thrashing he often punches holes in the wall. He shouts out bad words, smashing whatever is in his way. He is crying while he is doing this, which makes it very scary. It's very confusing.

Why is he crying?

I really think that I might be crazy and will go to Hell for what I think… and what I think about doing. My thoughts go so fast that I can't stay focused on anything. I wish I knew what I could do differently so he wouldn't hate me so much. It seems like I can't do anything that makes him happy.

I know my mom loves me, she always tells me to stay in my room when things are bad. I just can't do it. My mom says I need to be careful not to upset my father when he has been drinking. Even when he hasn't been drinking, we must be cautious. He can be set off easily. If his back is to us we need to quietly announce our presence to avoid a pretty scary reaction.

I try not to bother him. I can hardly breathe sometimes. My mom is so fragile with her illness. If she got hurt, it might kill her.

Please God, don't ever let that happen.

I don't think he will hit her because she is a girl. My father has told me that I better not ever hit a girl. But he does make her cry. That makes me cry.

I am so confused.

If I can think about baseball, sometimes it helps.

Why is he only like this when he gets drunk?

I am always worried that he doesn't know what he is doing.

I hate him, I wish I were bigger.

He has ruined my life, I will always be damaged.

I wish I had a huge scar across my face so someone would help me. I hate myself, there's something really bad about me.

What's wrong with me?

Sometimes I wish I were never born.

God doesn't even care.

Wha… what's that noise?

He's here…

CHAPTER TWO

Dragon's Roar
The Closet

Oh no, not again.

I can't do this!

This closet terrifies me.

I hear him yelling to my mom that she better get control of me.

I am so scared.

I can't even breathe right.

Dear God… Please help me stop crying.

Oh please! I need to stop acting like a baby.

I can't make any noise. Please don't cry.

What am I going to do?

I've tried biting the sleeve of my father's coat to muffle the sound, but I think he can still hear me.

What am I going to do?

Please let me try this …I hope this won't hurt too much.

Please let me do this.

I take one of the coat hangers from the coat rack, using the point of the hook, I stick it sharply to my skin near the corner of my eye.

Then… I slowly pull downwards to see how much pain I can tolerate.

Owwl….ooooow …..

Slowly… eventually the pain takes my breath away.
…hold it!…uhh,… …… …….................I'm not crying!
At least nobody can hear me.

CHAPTER THREE

SAFETY IN SILENCE
HOLD ON TIGHT

I'm holding myself tightly, disoriented and confused. I am not crying but wondering if my heartbeat or my breathing can be as loud as they feel. I've got to stay quiet.

I hear the walls rumbling as my father bounces from side to side heading towards his bedroom. After his door slams, my silence is swallowed as I wince and exhale to find a new breath. My heart continues to pound fiercely as I listen for what is next.

I hear whispering of my mom's voice from outside the closet. It scares me that my father might hear her. Through her tears, I hear her praying. She is praying to God, asking God to please help me remain quiet and to find peace. I pray but I'm careful not to make any noise.

Her voice is the only voice I trust. She tells me that she will let me out as soon as she is sure my father is settled.

My heart is calming, I open my eyes to see the darkness that surrounds me. My mom's voice touches something inside me that comforts my panic.

The door quietly opens, my mom's arms embrace me with her love. She softly speaks directly in my ear, "It is safe now, he's in his room."

As we sit cuddled on the couch, she reminds me that I need to stay away from my father when he has been drinking. She rubs my forehead and tells me she is sorry. When she softly rubs my forehead, I can think clearer.

She tells me it is alright to cry when I am with her. I know she is only trying to calm me down. She has tears in her eyes as she continues to hold me.

It hurts my heart and confuses my whole world.

I can't think about it for very long. I get very crazy thoughts.

It is better to be hurt than to be scared.

I know she is protecting me the only way she can. My mom explains that he doesn't mean to hurt or frighten me. She said he has problems that make him drink.

Sometimes I wondered if it was me that caused him to act like that. I was the one that would rush him, trying to make sure my mom would be safe. She had begged me to not attack him but to stay in my room.

I can't let my mom be hurt!

I have to do whatever I can.

As scared as I was of my father, he never hit me with his fists. He never even spanked me. I don't think he ever meant to hurt me.

He would push or toss me away, sending me flying. Sometimes he would grab me, holding me, shaking me to where I couldn't breathe. That was the worst. One time the side of my head caught the corner of a coffee table, drawing blood and leaving me with a black eye. That's the time that I had to tell my teacher and my friends that I slipped and fell. It was his yelling and the violent shaking of my body that would stay in my head and lead to my thoughts racing so fast that I couldn't sleep at night. Sometimes it helped if I slept under my bed.

I could never predict anything about my life. I had racing thoughts that were confusing and frightened me and I feared that I was crazy, so I felt that I had to hide what my thoughts were.

My father never hurt my brother. Maybe my brother really was asleep and truly didn't know what was happening. But sometimes I would hear him crying in his bed, though he always had his back to me, and his blanket was over his head. I think he had to know; he was just better at controlling his reaction. At this point in time my sister, Laura, was just a little baby – not even a year old. She slept in our mom's bedroom. I am pretty sure that she has no memory of the violent events. though I'm sure even infants feel that something is wrong.

I had another sister who was born and died when I was seven. Her name was Claire. I never saw or met her. She was only three days old and never came home from the hospital. I don't think we ever talked about her - if we did, I don't remember. I think my mom had a miscarriage when I was around two years old. I believe this only from pictures that I have seen of her pregnant holding me as an infant. We obviously never talked about this.

I had seen my father act so differently when he wasn't drinking. When he was nice to me, I would wonder if he remembered what he was like or what he did when he had been drinking. He was always nice when he wasn't drinking.

He taught me how to play baseball. I loved that time with him, but it could also be so confusing. I could never understand how I was supposed to respond to him. It was most confusing when I would hear and see a glimpse of tenderness and love from him.

My spot on those steps where I suffered so many fearful hours was the same spot on the steps where I witnessed a very different side of my father. From those steps, I was able to watch my father sitting on the couch playing his guitar and singing the songs that my mom loved. I could see her as she sat in that same flowery colored chair; her feet tapping lightly to the music and softly singing along with my father. She would be smiling.

It felt like they loved each other. It was a weird experience. It seemed like I wasn't supposed to be watching.

They couldn't see me, but I would smile when my mom would smile. I liked the way it made me feel. I wished it would last forever. Nobody could see me, I had a tear running down my cheek. I pinched it away.

It was a struggle within me. I didn't know how I was supposed to feel. Unfortunately, witnessing their beautiful, fleeting exchanges didn't make a difference to how I saw life or myself.

PART 2

CHAPTER FOUR

Weapons of Mass Destruction
Pain for Pain

The altercations with my father continued as his drinking remained problematic. My hateful thoughts of myself and my life, accelerated my self-abuse. It seemed to give me a sense of control and power.

Around age eleven or twelve, cutting myself with razor blades replaced the self-abuse that I had already mastered with coat hangers. I experimented cutting myself in different ways before I learned that cutting myself slowly so that I could feel the intensity of the pain, while watching for the release of my blood was most successful. It came easily to me.

This was how I would dissociate from my reality. As blood would leak from my body it gave me a sense of having control over something in my life. Of course, my actions didn't align with reality. Reality was what I didn't want. My actions were at a panic level; an obsessive fear of not having control over something in my life. In my distorted outlook, a false sense of control was better than the terror of no control.

My cutting was easy to conceal from others. These were all my choices. This was very private. It was my secret. My thighs were my favorite part of my body for cutting. I would hide the razor blades in my area of the closet, along with the big knife that I took from the kitchen. I would stick myself in my stomach with the kitchen knife, seeing how deep I could go. It hurt in a different way and didn't bleed as much so I didn't do it often.

I found that burning myself with cigarettes was another way to experience an altered feeling-state of numbness. The difference was that I didn't do this in secrecy. I would intentionally burn myself while in the company of others. I would place a lit cigarette against my arm, holding it until blistering and bleeding occurred. I would encourage others to watch, even challenging others to try to outlast how long they could hold the burning cigarette against their arm. I did this action to try to prove to them my toughness and craziness. In that time, this became my main disguise.

I had many ways of showing others that nothing could hurt me and that I was reckless and fearless. Fighting was another way that I covered up my constant fear of being discovered as the fearful, out of control boy that I saw in myself. I felt that I needed to influence how others saw and experienced me.

As I increased my self-injurious behaviors, it always reinforced the destructive lessons that I taught myself in the closet for so many years: that pain could relieve pain. This was a belief that I adhered to for way too many years.

I demonstrated this in all areas of my life. I believed I was a damaged person. Even my relationships were often sabotaged by me to avoid the chance of emotional vulnerability. I was always willing to hurt myself before you could hurt me.

Despite my harmful behaviors, I had always told myself that I would never drink alcohol and end up like my father. But my declarations didn't stop me from drinking when my life was spinning too fast, and I needed relief.

CHAPTER FIVE

Lost in a Masquerade
Dancing to Survive

At age fourteen, alcohol and drug use became my newest weapons of choice against the *Dragon*s. The first episode of my drinking ended with me being found by the police, passed out on the beach. I was only wearing my underwear and one sock. I still don't know the whole story.

Early on, my drinking revealed that I didn't drink like others. Not only because of the amount, but also because of the intent. I had no social motives in my usage. I just wanted to alter my mind as much as I could, as fast as I could. It was a slam dunk indicator of how loss of control was destined in my future. I never wanted normalcy with regard to altering my feeling state.

The destruction was gaining momentum. I wasn't using drugs and alcohol to feel better, I used drugs and alcohol to feel nothing. The wreckage continued throughout my high school years. Getting drunk or high was what I did every weekend. There were many car accidents, embarrassing incidents, disruptions in school… There was even a horror story of me doing some midnight surfing while tripping on LSD.

On the surface I was usually entertaining and always mysterious, just as I intended to be seen. I actually was pretty content with my new costumes and disguises. It felt comfortable and natural. I could even fool myself at times.

I didn't have to push people away with my gloom any longer. I was able to have fun with the aid of the substances. My masks and performances helped in making friends. I even tried to convince myself that I was likable and funny. My shame-based belief about myself told me that people were responding to my disguised self, not the real me. I retained the inner belief that if you really knew me, you would not like me. Even with all of the alterations I made to the way others saw me, my core beliefs of myself and life remained unchanged.

I felt like I had to try to figure out what others needed from me and I would do the best I could to be that person. That is why I wore so many masks.

CHAPTER SIX

OVER THE EDGE
IN AND OUT OF REALITY

Following my graduation from high school, I started college and got married. Within that same year, our first son was born. I was hoping that life would start to make sense and I would find a new pathway that I could trust.

The next year brought challenges from all directions: my mother died, my second son was born, my father died, and my wife's father died… all within the year.

I was questioning what was real and what was not. My *Dragons* were at full strength, now adding total memory blockage surrounding the reality of my parents' death to the arsenal of defenses. On some days I would believe my mother was still alive and only my father was dead. Other times, I thought just the opposite. Although I had experienced dissociative thoughts and actions for many years, these beliefs were extreme, and I feared total loss of reality. I attempted to silence some of the chaos of distortion through alcohol and drug use, though this only added flame to the fire.

I dropped out of school. I hated myself and was full of self-pity. This became the rationale for me to abandon my wife, my children, and my sister. When my wife and I divorced, I went to a new depth of darkness.

For the years to come I avoided my parental responsibilities. I actually avoided all responsibilities. I didn't want to die, though I didn't care if I lived. There were times I didn't know what was real and what was not. I thought my children would be better off without me. I feared that I would end up being like my father… or worse.

I found myself living in the reckless lane of cocaine and anything else that would keep me dancing fast enough to deny life's truth. I was in full costume and disguise where nothing was relevant or real.

My costumes changed as my lifestyle changed, from a homeless hippie to a flashy cocaine cowboy. I even spoke with a Spanish accent (I don't speak Spanish). I sought to be bizarre. I succeeded. Sometimes funny, sometimes scary, and always out of control. I was in a spiral of toxic glitz.

Self-hate poisoned my soul. My self-pity and shame were screaming. My self-hate was still partnered with my resentment towards my father.

You would think that my moral compass would have demanded change from me to bring a halt to the insanity. However, the many examples of the wreckage and mistakes never inspired me to change. The damages that occurred only reinforced the negative beliefs I'd had since I was a little boy.

I don't attempt to use this as an excuse, only as an example of how *Dragon*s, in the form of destructive self-talk, can distort and separate you from the ones that you love and value – your most precious people.

Continuing destructive behaviors in spite of adverse consequences in your life is a criterion of all addictions.

None of the shields and weapons that I used were ever successful in protecting me or improving my life. They only gave me the delusion of control. They would only give a temporary relief, always attempting to control or defeat my *Dragon*s.

In desperation, I came to a point where venturing outside the familiarity of my darkness seemed like the only alternative to succumbing to the fear and paranoia of my *Dragon*s. But that darkness had been with me since I was a little boy hiding in my bedroom closet. I found myself more afraid of the light than I was of the darkness that had been so much a part of my life for so long.

PART 3

CHAPTER SEVEN

Running to Escape
Desperation

Deciding that I needed to get out of that world, my new bride of four months and I packed up and hit the road.

I thought that leaving Florida and heading to Georgia would give me an opportunity to make the life changes that needed to happen. My new life venture was an attempt to stop using cocaine and gain some sense of manageability in my life. I hoped that by working a responsible job and making my new marriage work, I'd find love and happiness.

Sadly, my second marriage was shorter than my first. We mutually acknowledged that our relationship was solely about partying, dancing and mostly drug usage. We had no idea who each other really was or how we felt about each other. I thought we should just call it quits. She agreed. It was never a relationship that was based in intimacy and truth.

My second divorce brought about another version of the negative self-talk full of self-hate and self-pity.

There are way too many stories of wild craziness and dangerous life events. My life was a train wreck to say the least. I don't think it is necessary to include more examples of destruction. Too many "war stories" could take away from this book's purpose.

Of all places, I found a job working on the psychiatric unit at a large metropolitan hospital. I don't think it was a coincidence that I ended up working in the field of mental health and addiction. I had graduated from college a couple of years prior. I completed two internships at the psychiatric unit at the Veterans Hospital in Gainesville, Florida. I thought that the move and job would make a difference towards normalcy. I actually felt good about working with the psychiatric patient population. I liked going to work each day. Having a part in helping others was an amazing experience with challenges that provided life lessons as well as insights to ponder.

I was not attempting to stop drinking, just trying to limit it to the point where I could go to work and function with some success. It was my weekend adventures that remained a problem. My drinking, masks, and disguises weren't working. The audience was different. I also knew that it would just be a matter of time that I would be seeking cocaine or something else.

As life situations became stressful, my *Dragon*s continued to find their voice. I had the same negative self-talk chattering at me, as my mood was getting darker and gloomier. It seemed like depression and ideations of suicide were surrounding me, as I increasingly became preoccupied with thoughts of death. My compulsions were no longer about avoidance of truth or self-harm. It was no longer just about altering my feelings. At this point, my thoughts were saying that I might be better off dead.

My masquerade of glitter had lost its shine.

CHAPTER EIGHT

SEARCH FOR SANITY
I NEED HELP

Each day in my work I witnessed people that were seeking help with guidance from others. I saw myself in them and knew that I needed help but wasn't sure how to go about it. I was depressed and not able to hide from it like in the past.

I decided to find a therapist that I could trust and maintain my anonymity. I felt that I needed to be careful, fearing that if I revealed too much it would expose what a phony I had been all my life. I wanted to find a person that I could be honest and open with but still be able to maintain a safe sense of control.

After a few false starts, I realized that my relationship with my father prevented me from having a positive response to a male therapist. I went against recommendation and found an older female therapist with whom I felt comfortable. I hoped that she would be able to limit my manipulative ways and break through my defenses. I was ambivalent about letting anyone know the real me and I knew that I could be evasive and superficial. I was ambivalent about letting anyone know the real me.

I respected my therapist and slowly… reluctantly… ventured to talk about my history. It was a slow process, but eventually I was able to begin to share with her the events of my childhood.

At last I could tell someone what I believed destroyed my life. I started from the beginning and included all the ugly events of my past. Over many sessions I was able to be specific about what happened to me, but I refrained from telling her about how I felt and how I reacted to what happened.

Initially, my attempts to express my feelings were just statements of how I was confused and couldn't really tap into my feelings. My other frequent response was that I couldn't remember the events that well.

I did not tell her about my self-harm behaviors or my extreme destructive relationship with alcohol and drugs.

The consistent feedback from her was that I lacked emotional expression in my sharing. She said it was like I was talking about a movie that I had seen. Her feedback was like I was talking about someone else other than myself.

I knew what she was talking about. I had given many patients the exact same feedback, but somehow, I thought that my situation and life were different from that of my patients. I was trying to be open, but it was difficult.

My therapy appointments were always on Friday afternoon for a reason. For many, many months my routine was that I would follow each therapy session with a visit to a club or bar to deal with the backlash of my memories. I wouldn't tell my therapist that I was drinking following each session and throughout the weekend.

My progress was obsolete. My depression was actually worse. She was a good therapist and recognized that my sharing of the past, even as detailed and revealing as it was, wasn't improving my status. I still had occasional thoughts around the idea of suicide. It felt like my *Dragon*s were finally going to win.

My therapist continued encouraging me to move to, what she called, "a feeling level". I knew as well, that without the truth of my emotions, freedom from my conflicts would never happen. I did not intentionally refuse to go to the place where my emotions were restricted. Even from me, my defenses were hidden.

Blame and all the other *Dragon*s were the real blockades against my efforts. I had been working with my therapist for over a year and my lack of progress was very concerning for both of us. I needed to venture into a deeper level of truth or just give up.

Refusing to give up, I shared in detail what happened to me, describing my relationship with my father and his alcohol problems. I told her about the ways I attempted to protect myself from my feelings starting from the closet. The self-harm and drug and alcohol usage – past and present – were finally revealed in detail. I had never told anybody what I told her.

I also described in detail the love that I have for my mother and the loss I experienced with her death. We covered everything. I was hopeful that it would make a difference.

My list of conflicts and unresolved emotional stresses identified by my

therapist were:
- issues of abuse
- grief of my mother's death
- my father's death
- self-harm (drinking and drugging)
- relationship issues (abandonment of my children)
- low self-esteem
- sister and brother

She told me that her condition to continue to work with me would be that I must make an effort to stop drinking. She said that she would be enabling me without setting a boundary regarding my drinking. She gave me some different options to consider.

The option to go to Recovery meetings is what I agreed upon. I did not want to lose her in my life. I trusted, respected, and appreciated her. I knew she cared about me. I also knew that she was setting that boundary because she cared about me.

I feared that I would lose my job if they found out that I had problems with drugs and alcohol. My solution was to get a part time job at a private hospital that treated addiction. I served as an evening counselor and part of the job required me to drive patients to 12 Step meetings.

Mission accomplished. I honestly could tell my therapist that I was attending meetings.

I told myself that I would pay attention at those meetings and if there was anything I could relate to, I would entertain the idea to stop using and embrace their philosophies.

I needed to broaden my network for help and try to believe that I was worth saving.

PART 4

CHAPTER NINE

MOVEMENT TOWARDS TRUTH
SEEKING HUMILITY

I found meaning, purpose, and enjoyment in my part time job at the addiction treatment program. I was enlightened and inspired by working with the patient population, admiring their courage and openness. I recognized the characteristics of addiction and depression in myself and finally felt a sense of belonging.

I realized the compassion that I had for others was affecting me in a positive way. Even though I was developing compassion for the alcoholic, I remained ambivalent about my father. I understood that he was an alcoholic, like myself. Unfortunately, my resentments still haunted me. I had blinders on when it pertained to my father.

I took a full-time counselor position in the private mental health/addiction program. I was able to find empathy with others. I was experiencing genuine feelings with others without a need to filter and control my emotions and surroundings. I was able to be genuine in my efforts. I began attending recovery meetings as a participant, not as the driver. I began working with a sponsor in the recovery program. Something was starting to change. I told my therapist that I recognized I have an alcohol and drug problem and that I would work hard to refrain from using all substances. I stressed that I desperately wanted to find healing from my unresolved issues. My primary goal became being able to express my feelings with my heart, not my head. I felt good about my willingness and seemed to have a glimmer of real hope.

Despite my efforts I was not able to maintain abstinence for any significant period of time. My sponsor remained supportive and encouraging. I picked up a lot of white chips, the Surrender Chip at recovery meetings.

I was also honest with my therapist when I would relapse. She always remained supportive and willing to work with me as long as I was working a program of recovery with my sponsor. My therapist explained to me that my obvious blockage required a different approach and informed me that she was going to start using a different treatment technique in an attempt to open me to a deeper feeling state and free me from feeling so victimized by my past traumas. She would be using some experiential expressive methods to assist me. I knew that I needed to go there if I wanted to have a chance to change my life. She said my destructive self-talk should lessen if I could "unleash" my conflictual feelings. I was willing to try anything.

CHAPTER TEN

Force Against Force
Flaming the Fires

As I entered my therapist's office for our first session using the new approach, I was prepared to bare my soul. I observed a red foam bat resting next to the chair that I always occupied. I knew its purpose and was willing to go to work. I knew that this would be my opportunity to unleash the feelings that had been choking life from my soul.

These sessions went something like this:

Therapist:

"Thurman, you have done an excellent job of sharing with me your history. I appreciate you trusting me with all your secrets and sharing with me very specifically the experiences that have caused you problems."

"Today I want to look at that time in your life when your fathers drinking created so much chaos and pain for you. I hope you can allow yourself to tap into your feelings."

Try to relax as I ask you to revisit that time and what was happening. Then, when you feel ready, I want you to use the red foam bat as a vehicle to express your feelings."

Me:

"I know what that is, it's a Bataka Bat. I will try anything you want me to."

My therapist would go on and recap the story that I had shared many times of my father's rage and me in the closet.

She prompted me,

"Try to put yourself as a little boy, in the closet."

She went on to ask, "Now, see if you can experience what you are feeling."

I sat in silence for maybe twenty seconds and then I reached for the red foam bat. I looked up, connecting in eye contact with my therapist and started hitting the floor with the bat.

She nodded, and I slammed the bat, over and over, harder each time, YELLING!!

"Damn you! I hate you!"

(Swinging bat)

"Why did you do that?!"

(swinging harder and harder)

"How could you be such a monster?!"

I got louder, repeating my hate filled words, as tears filled my eyes. I swung the bat with rage from within. Harder!... Harder!!

"I HATE You!"

"I HATE YOU!"

(Over and over)

Therapist:

"How do you feel? You just released a lot."

Me:

"Exhausted, I feel better though. I'm glad I could do that."

I was shaking, feeling strange, like a familiar confused feeling state of my past.

As I exited my therapist's office, the receptionist, Sandy, was smiling at me; her hands in a silent clapping motion. She even had a tear leaking down her cheek. I was proud of my effort and everyone else seemed to feel the same.

I would drink on my way home.

This continued and even worsened as the sessions continued. I kept trying. I yelled and dreamed, beating and beating with all my force. Tears would even flow. Same outcome.

If I didn't drink on Fridays, most often it would happen on Saturday nights. My depression and hopelessness increased.

My therapist was concerned with my lack of progress and suggested that we change my focus. She acknowledged the good work I was doing but felt like I needed to face my feelings for my mother, this time not to involve the Bataka bat.

Therapist:

"Thurman, you have told me many times about how much you love your mother. You have described her so beautifully; your love is so obvious. We have talked about her death, and you have stated that you have difficulty remembering anything about it."

"I would like you to close your eyes, picture your MOTHER and I would like you to tell your MOTHER how much you love her and then share with me how you feel about her not being in your life any longer."

Me:

"I love you mom. I have always loved you with all my heart and always will."

(Pause)

"Why did God take you so soon?"

(tears)

"Why did you have to suffer so much"

(tears)

"Dad shouldn't have made you worry like you did."

(tears)

"I shouldn't have made you worry."

(tears)

(tighter clenched fist)

"I should have been a better son."

(tears)

"It's not fair, you're the only person that ever loved me!"

(tears and clenched fists)

"I hate my life; I'll never be happy."

I cried buckets and buckets of tears.

This time, there was no clapping from Sandy, although there was an exchange of tenderness in her goodbye.

With all that, and even my own sense of accomplishment, I really wanted to use something to make me feel different.

During the next session, my therapist again asked me to talk about being in the closet. She asked me to express the emotions that I experienced while in the closet.

I eventually reacted by sharing the beliefs that served to protect me. It was like a reflex to blame my father, shame myself, or blame God.

I left feeling anxious and with racing thoughts. Something was different! I kept thinking about myself as a little boy.

I did hear what I said when she asked me what it was like in the closet. It sounded the same, but something felt very different.

I realized that I avoided expressing what I felt while I was in the closet.

I was coming to realize and recognize what my defenses were guarding against.

It was extreme sadness, fear, and anger that a nine-year-old had to escape from.

I was frightened and feared dying.

CHAPTER ELEVEN

Recognizing the Enemy
Self-Exposed

I can't explain why or how, but I finally recognized *Dragons* for what they really were: my defensive, dysfunctional, self-talk.

Something helped me to realize that what I thought was expressing my emotions from my trauma, was actually only me repeating my thoughts, beliefs, and judgments about my father and the events of my life.

With every swing of the Bataka exclaiming rage towards my father, my *Dragon*s became stronger and stronger. I was not releasing pain or anger. I was repeating the reasons my life was damaged, inflaming my wounds.

For all my exhausting efforts put into that Bataka bat, every swing that I made was really only me blaming God, my father, and myself. Instead of spending that time purging myself of anger I was really just complaining about what shouldn't have happened… over and over again.

My judgments and blaming were the poison that fed my *Dragon*s; the same voices of self-centered fear that seemed to be tethered to all my chaos.

When asked to express my emotional feelings about my mother being dead, self-pity and judgment were always present as I expressed that my mother shouldn't have died. I would cry that it was unfair, blaming God, myself, and my father.

Self-centered shame, resentment, and pity are just different types of poison with the same dysfunctional outcome.

When I finally identified my *Dragons*, conclusions were revealed that distinguished *Dragons* from real emotions:

- A *Dragon* always includes a JUDGMENT. Emotions never do.
- Blame is the biggest defense against truth.

Recognizing the Enemy

- *Dragons* can fool anyone, even you.
- *Dragons* look and sound like emotional truth.
- *Dragons* have many disguises.
- Being able to recognize a *Dragon* is the beginning of the path to freedom.
- Emotional truth still needs to be expressed, otherwise the *Dragons* will get stronger.
- All feelings have purpose. Even the uncomfortable ones.
- *Dragons*' attempt to keep you fearful of intimacy.
- *Dragons* do anything and everything to distort reality.
- *Dragons* can look and sound like a healthy emotional release.
- *Dragons* want you to fight against them.
- *Dragons* use the force applied against them, against you.

CHAPTER TWELVE

Here Comes the Sun
Divine Interventions

Work continued to be a bright spot as I found passion and a sense of worth working with the people in the recovery environment. I had stopped using alcohol and drugs. The work I had finally set in motion with my therapist was starting to make a difference in my life. I had cried and vented everything inside of me. I was able to continue with my participation in my recovery meetings and started making friends with people that sounded and looked a lot like me.

My sponsor, who served as a mentor in helping me work the program of recovery, was a retired chicken farmer from Gainesville, Georgia. Having only a fourth grade education, he started working in the chicken industry when he was fifteen years old. He became financially very successful, retiring at age fifty. When I met him, he was probably in his early seventies and he was twenty-four years sober.

He is the one who probably had the most profound impact in helping me recognize some necessary truths against which I had allowed my *Dragon*s to fend off and distort. He had a way of keeping everything as simple as possible, which came out as gems of wisdom. There was even an old rocking chair at the meeting house which, somewhere along the way, had been deemed as "his chair."

Despite making some progress in freeing myself from my *Dragon*s, I wasn't exactly happy, joyful, or free by any means. My sponsor told me that it was great that I wasn't using, but cautioned me against stopping my work with my therapist.

One memorable night, something happened that provided a clarity that affected me as a "Divine Intervention."

Thanksgiving was approaching. The holidays were times that I was known to volunteer to work extra at my place of employment and at my Recovery meetings.

The speech I would give sounded something like this:

"As you all know, I have lost my relationship with my children because of my addiction and will be available to help in any way I can."

In the midst of this generous offering, I heard from the back of the room, where his rocking chair settled, a voice interrupting my own... his voice...

"When are you going to quit feeling sorry for yourself, shut up and take responsibility and go see your children?"

I was shocked... even angry.

I couldn't believe that he said that to me in front of the entire group. My first thought was that he just doesn't understand my situation. Then, I noticed that there were many other people nodding their heads in agreement.

That interruption was a breakthrough that opened to new insights. My experiences with my therapist were being replayed over and over. Hoping to free myself from the associated self hate, I had told myself that I had owned my guilt and shame over abandoning my children. I had cried and even screamed to release that pain. I thought I was making progress.

"What else did I need to do?"

"Was my sponsor right? Do I sound like I have self pity and act like a victim?"

After the meeting, I sought him out to have a conversation outside on the porch.

As it turned out, he did all of the talking. In his way, he kept it short, simple, and left me with a gem of wisdom.

Sponsor:

"If you ever expect to stop feeling guilty about abandoning your kids, GO BE THERE FOR YOUR KIDS!"

With that, he gave me a hug, turned, and walked to his car.

That changed my life.

There were other things that suggested the work I had done with my therapist wasn't finished. As my sponsor would remind me, "The work you do with a therapist and the work of our Recovery groups are the same stuff, just using different words." There was a greater opening of truth happening.

The guidance I was receiving was coming from all directions. Some dots were starting to connect.

As a case manager at work, I also had the opportunity and responsibility to work with the patients' family members. This gave me many opportunities for valuable lessons. As is depicted in the below Case Summary, one of these was the opportunity to have an experience that taught me a powerful lesson about emotional truth.

Case Summary:

Patient is a twenty-four year old female that was transferred to our facility from Fulton County Jail. She has been charged with sexual solicitation and possession of narcotics.

As a condition of her probation she is required to complete a ninety day treatment program for her addiction to heroin.

With our first meeting she reported that she had been through three prior treatment programs. She stated, "I have been through all this crap many times! It will be a waste of time but I know I need to be here."

She openly shared her history of drug usage, her legal history, and a history of sexual abuse by her father. She added that she has talked about her issues over and over.

She reported that in her second treatment program her therapist required that she have a family session including her father and mother. She said the meeting was "pure hell."

She said that she confronted her father of the sexual abuse and called him every name in the book. She said that he just sat there with a grin on his face. She reported that her father completely denied her accusations and told her she was crazy.

She said that when she confronted her mother for ignoring what was happening for all of those years, her mother responded by scolding her for dressing like a, "little whore." Her mother said that she would pray to God to change her sinful ways.

She said the only thing that the meeting accomplished was it helped her realize that her life would always be a living hell. She said, "I am damaged goods and always will be."

She reported that two days after her discharge from treatment she ended up in an Emergency Room from the result of a heroin overdose.

In our first counseling session she said that the sexual abuse started when she was thirteen years old and continued until age sixteen. That was when she ran away from home, never to return. She reported that she supported herself by selling drugs, a bit of lingerie modeling, and selling her body for money or drugs.

She said, "my body has already been ruined, so none of that stuff bothers me."

As I listened to her story I could not help but to relate to my own life situation.

Her situation was different… but, somehow, the same.

She said that she started drinking and doing drugs around age fifteen, adding that she tried being bulimic but it never seemed to work. She told me she sometimes still cuts herself and punches herself in the face when drinking or drugs are not available. She said that she hoped I wouldn't put her in a lock down "nut ward" for telling me.

I recognized her shame; how she saw herself as a disgusting person. I also recognize her rage and anger towards her father… blaming him for her current life situations. Mostly, I really recognized her self destructive behavior and her lack of hope for the future.

I could clearly see that she needed to stop engaging in attempting to resolve her rage against her father and expecting him to acknowledge or apologize for his actions. Her mother and father denied everything that happened. She needed to accept that she could not change anything about them, or what happened in the past.

As tragic and sad as what happened to her was, she needed to not let what and who caused her trauma to continue to define her identity and her life.

I was humbled and fortunate to help her to distinguish her toxic beliefs of herself from her real self. What touched me so spiritually from this experience was that I had never articulated these insights prior to this time. The guidance was for the both of us and was definitely a power greater than either of us.

Together in individual therapy, we had worked on the differences between expressing emotions about what happened versus expressing judgment about who did it.

She had been in treatment for around forty days when I suggested that we have a meeting with her family. She agreed, accepting the probability that they would continue to deny the abuse and continue to blame her as their defense.

The family session was conducted and she was able to state her feelings about being sexually abused. She was able to express anger and sadness of the abuse happening and how her blaming rage and her own self hate had fueled her self destruction.

She avoided making any blaming statements towards her father and mother.

As predicted, her mother and father continued to deny the abuse, stressing their point of her being crazy and a liar. Her mother couldn't resist adding that she would continue to pray for her.

After the session, the young woman shared with me that she was grateful that she no longer expected an acknowledgement or apology from her parents. She stated, "My parents are not the subject of my emotional truth… I am."

The patient remained calm, with her tears, not of pain, but sadness in grief. She made eye contact with me and actually smiled. She said her tears actually felt calming to her. She said she knew that she had lots of work and change ahead of her. She said that, for the first time, she wanted to change and believed she could.

She thanked me for my help. I thanked her for her courage and for trusting me with her truth.

By being a part of her journey I received as much as I gave. Something touched me that gave me a beautiful burst of hope.

God is good.

When I told my sponsor about this exchange, he smiled and simply said, "That's how it works, you get what you give."

Could it really be that simple?

One year later, the young woman that I presented in the case study above celebrated one year sober and I had the honor of giving her a beautiful blue chip.

CHAPTER THIRTEEN

HEALING IN GOD'S WILL
SURRENDER TO WIN

My therapy sessions started to move in a positive direction. My therapist didn't change, I did. The difference was that I started to share my emotional feelings, avoiding the blockages of resentments, shame and self pity.

What I eventually learned about my *Dragon*s was that their initial arrival was intended to protect me from the intensity of the trauma that was overwhelming. This was an involuntary survival technique that came into action to protect me from distress. They were successful as a defense mechanism in regard to distracting me from my terror; the problem was in some situations the actions, interpretations and conclusive beliefs were sometimes not founded in logic, creating pain to divert from pain. That is what defined my compulsions to alter my feeling state. That was a serious problem. My insights and ability to recognize these *Dragon*s, made staying with my emotions become more natural.

Being able to feel the unguarded emotions and being able to express them was the opening of my healing. I still had lots of work to do but the challenges were now being revealed where I could identify my realistic responsibilities.

*Dragon*s are tricky, the longer they exist the more powerful they become. They are based in the past, blocking your presence in the present. When self-talk is corrupted by fear it can kidnap your spirit. Resentment and blame of anything, judging that it shouldn't have happened sounds and looks like a healthy expression of anger. Unfortunately it actually agitates oneself, increasing the unresolved feeling. An example of this was when I was asked to express how I felt about being abused by my father when I was young, I could easily shout, I hate him, how could he do what he did to me? I can't believe he made my mother worry so much. Those are examples of expressing my judgment about what happened instead of sharing how I felt about it happening to me. Why? is a question that kept me sick for a very long time. My need to know Why? was the core of my resentment about what happened to me in the closet. It was my judgment that what happened, shouldn't have happened. Why? was my judgment about my father, again, a way of avoiding my feelings of what happened to me.

Realizing and truly feeling about what happened to me was not about my father, or my mother. It was just the truth of feeling the terror that I experienced being in the closet. Fear was the core feeling that possessed me about my mother dying that would leave me alone, unable to exist without her. I was able to vent the intensity of the terror, able to find freedom from my resentments, shame and self pity. To realize that my life is based on the truth of the moment.

Trauma is real. There are many things that happened that are unfortunate. It was sad about what happened to me and I obviously had a full range of conflicted emotions about those events. Whatever the cause was, whether it is old or new, it needs intervention for you to achieve emotional stability and freedom in your life. Intervention does not mean defeat, cure, overcome, let go, turn it over, or get rid of. Victory comes in the form of developing a different relationship with the conflict. You will always have feelings, feelings are never the problem.

Grief acts in the same way. It is helpful to understand that detaching from the battle with a *Dragon*, is when emotional truth can exist.

For many years there were many truths that I couldn't accept. I didn't realize that love was always around me. I couldn't feel and receive it because all my versions of self-centered blame blocked it.

When I realized that *Dragon* self-talk was the driving source of my dysfunction, I realized that I actually had options that could free me from their fury. Learning that it was my choice to not engage with a *Dragon* was my opening to my willingness to seek guidance with faith as my source.

You are not always the only one that is responsible for your beliefs. Although I was the primary author of my negative self talk, many times messages of shame or blame are delivered by others. This is why issues of negative self worth require challenging the validity of our core beliefs.

Belief in yourself is not just something that you convince yourself of. Belief in yourself is based on your existence in the truth and your relationship with it.

For many years there were many truths that I couldn't accept. I didn't realize that love was always around me. I couldn't feel and receive it because all my versions of self-centered blame blocked it.

One of my biggest obstacles I faced was that I saw my father as a *Dragon*. Reality is that My father was not a *Dragon*. Although his actions did cause trauma, I stress that "*Dragon*s" are the consequences of unresolved trauma. My father was an alcoholic. He had a disease that was obviously driven by a herd of his own "*Dragon*s."

When I accepted that my father was not his disease. I was able to forgive him in the same way that I came to forgive myself. Being able to realize and express that I love my father and that he loved me, was a healing of my spirit that made me view life completely differently. It didn't happen suddenly, definitely not a "white light" experience. It was more like a gradual consciousness of the presence of the guidance that surrounds me.

I am grateful for where my past has brought me. Though my ride was bumpy for sure, my journey has become a wonderful, spiritual awakening.

I came to realize and accept my powerlessness against resentment, shame and self pity. I needed to feel and share my feelings of being a terrorized, confused, fearfully sad child.

I didn't need to yell and scream about who or why. I had done that for most of my life. I was needed and was able to express my emotions in truth. The difference was that it wasn't directed toward my father or God. It was my feeling about me. Giving up the blaming clears the pathway to my true emotions.

My mother's death was my most difficult truth to face. The defense that opposed me was absolute avoidance. I denied the reality that she had passed, I would do anything I could to avoid even thinking about her. I told myself that I would lose my mind and never get it back. Anything that reminded me of her was a signal to distract myself from thoughts and memories of her. Blocking my soul from feeling her presence.

Unlocking those defenses, allowed me to feel the sadness in truth. As painful as they were, it allowed me to feel God. To feel the glory of living in truth.

Those feelings are what inspired my soul to continue to embrace my truth. My new found tears washed away the darkness that the *Dragons* had cast over my memories for so many years. The light was shining through. I could breath without fear. I felt a rush of love that I had long forgotten, as the tears ran down my cheek. There was joy mixing with the tears and I could see and feel excitement as my memory of my mother opened.

There she was, holding my baby sister gracefully in her arms, the beauty of her smile highlighting the giggles from my sister, Laura. She danced lightly across the living room floor, her bedroom slippers made a swishing sound that provided the music. There was no need for lyrics, God's melody was present.

The same room that was the shadow of so much pain, so much fear, was now the canvas of the reunion of my mother and my heart. I could see and feel her again. Her smile would always comfort me. She had a twinkle in her eyes that could see me like no others could. Her cry in her tender whisper told me she loves me and that everything will be alright. The most beautiful touch to my heart ever. At that moment I knew she was happy, healing something inside of me that I can't label. An intoxicating caress to my soul that profoundly allowed God's grace to be realized and embraced.

I smiled as I remember, if she wasn't sick, that she always made sure she arrived early for mine or my brother's baseball games. She would always be sitting on the second row-end of the bleacher seat. She made sure that her purse was stocked with plenty of bubble gum for the team and even some tootsie roll candy for me while I went through a time, around age ten, that sticking a wad of the gooey candy in my mouth to spit the chocolate juices was a good alternative to what the major leaguers were doing. I remember that I did laugh and have fun like other kids, and I wasn't faking it.

Memories of my father came along as well. I had blocked those memories also.

I felt the healing in my tears as I recalled many times spotting my dad down the left field line, leaning against the fence as he watched me playing. I don't ever remember him sitting in the bleachers but he was there. My feelings were always ambivalent. My heart has healed but there are scars that are tender to the touch that remain. He taught me to play baseball, even coached at times. Those were probably our closest times. I'm pretty sure he was proud of me.

These memories are evidence that my *Dragons* distorted my good memories along with the bad ones.

After years of hiding in darkness I was able to step into the light without fear of breaking. The light that I refer to is the presence of God's pure loving energy. My soul finally found peace through acceptance. This freedom softened the pressure that had been squeezing my chest seemingly forever,

A genuine smile often accompanies my tears. Real raw emotions are now cherished and honored. I now celebrate the opportunity for memories and other reminders that visit my mind and spirit.

I still miss my mother and experience the full range of emotions of her not living long enough to ever meet the special loves of my life; to see me in my beauty of God's light.

That's because grief and love work that way. Love is everlasting in our hearts. Truth revealed that what I feared would destroy me was really what strengthens my faith and continues to guide me.

My tears are tears laced with love not pain. They serve as a channel of precious feelings and memories that I hid from for many years. My tears actually gave me a profoundly beautiful sense of love. I came to honor and find gratitude in my grief. That allows me to stay in the presence of now. Living life in sync with life's actions.

I learned through my journey that grief is not a negative, punishing feeling state. Grief is a path of truth to find gratitude in memory that is validation of shared love. Those feelings are what inspired my soul to continue to embrace my truth.

As for me continuing to attempt to change anything from my past, I like to say that I am retired from doing that. It is understandable to have these wishes. They are unfortunately unattainable. Resentments separate one from the reality of the present. To wish something didn't happen, that did happen, is delusional.

Acceptance is an act of living in the present and in truth with God's will. Acceptance of the things you cannot change, is profound wisdom.

All my issues of my childhood conflict were eventually addressed with me being able to express my emotions productively, staying free from my self centered beliefs and judgments. My new relationship with emotions is based on honoring their existence. This transformation along with the guidance from every person and life experience connected me with the presence of grace, turning my darkness into light. This was how I was able to embrace my relationship with God, self, and others. I could feel my feelings, most wonderfully I could feel the love from others and share my feelings towards others. There is purpose in all feelings.

Finding the major distinction of the difference between emotions and judgments was alacrity that saved my life. My life completely changed in all areas. It didn't happen suddenly, definitely not a "white light" experience. It was more like a gradual consciousness of the presence of the guidance that surrounds me. I came to realize change had constantly been in movement. Finally experiencing the beauty and love that always had been there.

"I am not damaged, and never have been." I was not bad, wrong or weak in my actions and behaviors as a child. I did the best I could in attempting to handle my life at that time.

I came to realize change had constantly been in movement. Finally

Healing in God's Will

experiencing the beauty and love that always had been there. I now believed it was there, I just needed to feel, look, and listen for it.

I found true relationship with others and life by connecting these new insights, emotions and behaviors. It changed my perception of everything. My self talk was different, finding trust in myself and others. I became able to exchange feelings in truth, finding intimacy with people and life in whole. I no longer see myself as greater than, or less than. I am gratefully, humbly, simply a part of something bigger and greater in God's purpose.

CHAPTER FOURTEEN

GIVING TO RECEIVE
GIFT EXCHANGE

When my *Dragon*s of self-centered will no longer defined my identity and my life, my spiritual path led me towards a new life in God's Grace. Healing doesn't require the absence of discomfort, only the freedom from victimization.

This change wasn't solely due to the silencing of the *Dragon*s. Of course that was a hugely significant factor, though it was the behavioral actions of change (living amends) that led to enlightenment.

It was exactly the same process that my sponsor taught me when he suggested that if I ever expected to rid myself of shame of my role as a father, I needed to quit my negative self pity, shaming, self-talk and be responsible and go see my children. Change requires action.

I learned that my self worth isn't defined by belief, but by actions. My prayer was for myself to give to others in genuine truth and receive in God's will. Through guidance received, I hoped to give in all areas of my life.

"Giving is how we are open to receive. Receiving and embracing to our soul directs us to give."

This truth continues to be the formula for my spiritual condition. Living in the present is our most spiritual action of embracing Grace. With my shame, resentments and self pity absent, living in the present was possible and full of rewards.

Contrary to some beliefs on love of self, it started with me giving love to others before I could love myself. Self affirmations and attempts to change my belief of myself never worked for me. I had to go with a leap of faith and give love, trusting the outcome. I gave love and love came my way.

Because the love that I gave was of emotional truth, {not with a motive to protect myself or manipulate, as in my past} I trusted the exchange and allowed my soul to feel the beauty.

In my past I thought love and any real possibility of happiness died when my mother died. I thought God had abandoned me.

The base of all my changes and my life rewards are based in love.

It is the essence of what I call God's Grace. "God is Love, Love is God."

I wish I could say everything was like rainbows and puppy dogs, never a problem again. Of course, I can't. Life can be cruel. Life can be unfair. Lots of life reasons for *Dragon*s to appear. This is where faith shines.

What I am grateful for is that I can recognize the *Dragon*'s roar, I not only turn the negative roar down, I most effectively turn the volume up of what is precious in my life. Taking a daily inventory is an affirmative action that actually is an enlightening process that strengthens your connection with God.

My own personal trauma is something I have come to not regret but to embrace as a pathway to faith. My life experiences found a channel to connect with other people that have gone through similar tragedies and events. This is an outcome of emotional truth, it's like a spiritual magnet.

CHAPTER FIFTEEN

Treasures of the Heart
Embracing Grace

For me it was not about loving myself before I could love anyone else. My destructive self talk would never allow that. It was from my actions of love from me given to others that affirmed my God given love of myself. That had always been God's Will, I just always blocked it with my self centered will. Belief in yourself is not just something that you convince yourself of. It is your current existence in life's truth that has always been there.

Looking at life through lenses of truth allowed me to open all my senses to the beauty of God's beauty in all that surrounds me. I am not referring to perfection, but in life's imperfection as well. Openness and willingness are active efforts of the quest to connect with God's will.

With these newly found realizations I learned that love didn't have to hurt. I felt a peace in my soul that had been evading me. I ventured into life from a place of faith, not fear.

Being able to embrace my blessings of my current life existance, accepting that my life journey had purpose and provided enlightenment through truth. Along with embracing the love and support given to me, allowed me to give love in full exchange, dancing in the light of God's Grace.

My life changes brought my sons from my first marriage back into my life. Their mother, one of my life heroes, raised them as a single parent for most of their childhood. Wounds needed healing but my hope and faith was strong. They needed a father, and I needed to start to be accountable.

I couldn't change the past but I wanted to make a difference in the present with my acts of making living amends. Self forgiveness can only exist from my adherence to change.

My sister and brother were again in my life in full. We found each other with eagerness to embrace without blame. We had only lost our way, never our love. Healing was beginning to happen in all areas of my life.

I found love in a marriage that held a dream. Allowing me to trust and to find intimacy in being vulnerable. Real love. Revealing myself in a personal relationship was new to me. I was a 33-year- old rookie. It changed everything. Love healed my soul. God is love.

God's most creative gifts happened in 1982. [January and November]

Two precious earth angels were gifted to me and my wife.

The challenges and rewards of parenting was the most profoundly healing experience in my life. My childhood wounds around not feeling loved by my father, somehow lost their sting. Giving love to those babies opened the channel to the love I was able to share throughout all areas of my life. Being able to realize and express that I love my father and that he loved me, was a healing of my spirit that made me view life completely differently.

It's amazing how teaching and caring for children ends up giving you clarity of purpose in life. As a husband and parent I also exchanged joy, laughter and tears through our love.

It was my honor to participate in my children's life in full. I was able to coach children in baseball and football, I got to watch "Grease" at least 20 times, and even learned some cheerleading chants and routines. I loved it all. It was love that very powerfully caressed my spirit, releasing a weight that had burdened me forever. My experiences of parenting taught me so many life lessons that led me to healings and to self forgiveness.

My friends and family's love and caring surrounded me. When grandchildren arrived it was like hitting the emotional lottery. All relationships of love were where God's exclamation points. I could go on and on, bragging about each of them. So many examples of the presence of God in my life.

Being connected, being a part of something/someone greater, other than myself was the profound factor of my salvation. My ability to give love allowed me to feel and trust love from others.

The voice of my story had seriously changed. The history was the same, my past was my past. What had changed was that I spoke to myself differently. My current self-talk was based on the here and now. I no longer defined myself on the beliefs that I took on as a 9 year old, lost and confused child. Those beliefs fueled my past dysfunction.

My life is now present in the moment with lifes truth as my guidance. I embrace life in hope and faith, looking and listening for the grace that surrounds me.

EPILOGUE

Writing this book has meant many different things to me, most profoundly the need to maintain hope and faith throughout the healing process. Even though the roar has lessened and a sense of freedom is present, healing can have many layers and even disguises.

Healing is not about stopping or controlling the pain. Pain is actually the indicator and compass for the pathway to find the peace and freedom that defines healing. Not feeling can be a sign of an ugly *Dragon*, be careful. The absence of destructive behavior is a more accurate demonstration of healing.

The biggest and most appreciated area of my ongoing growth and healing pertained to my feelings of my father. For at least the last twenty-five years, I had sincerely found healing in acceptance and forgiveness of my father. I thought I had obtained freedom from those blaming, shaming *Dragon*s and thought my work was done in that area. My father has been dead for over fifty years.

In time, keeping my emotional channel open, connected me in empathy with him in the presence of love. I came to realize that my father always loved me and I always loved him. We both were separated from our truths by distorted stories of our illnesses. It never was our choice, never was our

Retired Dragon Fighter - Epilogue

fault.

My awakening was actually very beautiful. I was able to separate the man that terrorized me, with a man that obviously fought his own, uninvited *Dragons*. I know now his rage was towards himself. The same *Dragons* I fought.

I was given the blessing of compassion towards my father as I sought to deliver compassionate actions with others in all areas of my life. These actions found spiritual fulfillment exhibited in my welcoming of love that affirmed a positive belief of my self worth. My own tears of love embraced me as I was able to recognize his love for me. My actions of love towards my own children led the way, helping me to realize my father's love for me. Love opened truths to me that I thought I would never experience. It is really cool how that happens.

Hopefully, sharing my experience, strength, and hope, highlights the importance of living in the present as part of something greater than yourself, embracing the beauty and love that surround you.

Healing isn't something we do. Healing is something that happens.

~Thurman Strother

Encountering a Dragon

A PARABLE BY
THURMAN STROTHER & ALLE BYESEDA

PROLOGUE

Our primary purpose of writing this book is to inspire people to trust that all emotions have a purpose to our healthiest self. All emotions are helpful and positive, even the uncomfortable ones. They are meant to align with our life realities, maintaining our spiritual balance.

REMINDER: *Dragon*s are NOT emotions! They are self-talk stories arriving to keep you from the intensity of your emotional truths.

Even the less obvious *Dragons* such as impatience, intolerance, jealousy and boredom are self centered wishes or complaints that something isn't the way it should [according to you] be.

Nobody is perfect, Everyone has self-talk stories that are often very convincing in content. It is necessary to face the *Dragon*, not acknowledging what's happening and not willing to embrace the intensity of emotional truth is harmful.. Trying to deny a *Dragon* would require a harmful level of defense that would lead to a silent *Dragon* that is even more destructive.

Facing a *Dragon* doesn't mean engagement. It doesn't mean trying to defeat it. Facing your *Dragon* is courageously realizing the distinction between truth based emotions vs. self talk of your blaming judgment. This breaks the bondage the *Dragon* seeks.

Even though you have power over many difficult challenges, there are challenges that you are powerless over. Avoid fighting to defeat unchangeable obstacles that result in adverse consequences using your unrealistic efforts against you. Use your strengths only against opponents that exist in the present truth. Seek and embrace what is most precious in your life.

SUGGESTIONS: Read the parable out loud with somebody you love. This will reveal insights and purpose to a different level. SHARING is what makes it a spiritual exchange. Interaction with others is what unites the spirits and releases love.

List of Characters:

The Handsome Prince

In writing the story the Handsome Prince represents me. As the reader, the Prince is YOU (non-gender specific).

The Beautiful Princess

Represents everything that is precious to us.

Examples:
People I love and who love me
My connection to God and all my life values and principles.

The Dragon

Represents destructive judgmental self-talk that is based in self-centered fear, diverting from the truth of self and life.

Examples:
shame, resentments, self pity, blaming God, self, or others.

The Wizard

Represents the voice of truth. Guidance from a source that is not distorted from self-centered will.

The Sorcerer

Represents the incident of trauma or conflict.

Encountering a Dragon

A PARABLE BY
THURMAN STROTHER & ALLE BYESEDA

A PARABLE

Encountering A Dragon

There once was a beautiful Princess that lived in the Northern Kingdom of Loveland. She was deeply in love with the handsome Prince that lived in the Southern Kingdom of Loveland on the other side of a deep, dark, scary forest. The two kingdoms had been divided for as long as anyone could remember, but the love between the Princess and the Prince brought hope for a United Kingdom of Loveland when the two decided to get married.

Within the deep, dark, scary forest lived an evil Sorcerer. As fate would have it, the night before the big wedding day, the evil Sorcerer snuck into the castle of the beautiful Princess and captured her. With the beautiful Princess as his prisoner, the evil Sorcerer made way to his dark, dungy castle as he vanished into the cover of the fog that cloaked the night forest.

The next day when the Queen and King awoke, they realized that their daughter had been taken. Terrorized, they sent a rider to the castle of the Prince to call for his aid.

When the rider arrived at the castle in the Southern Kingdom, he told the prince that the sucpicion was that the Princess had been kidnapped by the evil Sorcerer. The handsome Prince grabbed his mighty hammer and

A Parable

shield, mounted his big white horse and raced through the kingdom gates to rescue the beautiful Princess.

Arriving at the Princess's Northern castle, he searched for evidence to assist his quest. He found horse tracks under her castle window that led towards the evil Sorcerer's dark, dungy castle in the deep, dark, mysterious forest. The handsome Prince knew that going up against the evil Sorcerer would not be easy. The evil Sorcerer was infamous for his trickery and deceipt, but the handsome Prince was prepared. So, unless it was a Dragon (which the handsome Prince had never seen), he felt confident that he would overcome whatever obstacles the evil Sorcerer might have set up along the way. With that, the handsome Prince did what any handsome Prince would do and set off on his quest to rescus the beautiful princess.

The first challenge the evil Sorcerer put before the handsome Prince was a group of twenty archers, shooting flaming arrows as they hid behind the forest trees. Being the handsome Prince that he was, he took up his shield and blocked the flaming arrows as they hurled towards his path. Gripping his mighty hammer, he continued to go forth as he defeated the twenty archers.

The handsome Prince continued his quest to rescue the beautiful Princess. His next challenge came when he had to take on fifty men armed with spears and lances, charging from all directions at full speed.

The handsome Prince, being the powerful warrior that he is, defeated all fifty men. The handsome Prince, ever so powerful and strong, remained determined to rescue the beautiful Princess. There was nobody as powerful as the handsome Prince!

As the Prince went further into the forest he came upon a pathway to the dark, dungy castle that obviously belonged

Encountering a Dragon

to the evil Sorcerer. As he got closer to the castle he could see a gate that would provide entrance to the castle. As he rode closer to the entrance he tightened his grip on his hammer and shield, steadying himself to take on whatever might stand in his way. As he made his way through the castle gate, he saw a gigantic outline of something looming up ahead; positioning itself to block the entrance to the castle. As he continued to approach, he knew that it could only be one thing: a huge, fiercely growling, flame spitting DRAGON!

The handsome prince had been terrified of dragons ever since he was a little boy. He fretted that if he ever came upon a dragon he would not be able to defeat it, so he had convinced himself that dragons were not real and he trained day in and day out for his entire life to become the strongest warrior in all the land. He had already defeated the twenty archers and the fifty armed men but, even as strong and powerful as he was, facing this dragon crippled him with fear.

The handsome Prince pulled back hard on the reins of the horse, coming to a complete stop. His whole body was shaking and he was TERRIFIED! A little voice inside of his head reminded him of his childhood fear of dragons, and told him that he would never be able to defeat this big, mean, scary Dragon.

Yet, the handsome Prince loved the beautiful Princess, and he knew that he simply *had* to rescue the beautiful Princess. And in order to rescue the beautiful princess, he knew now that he MUST defeat this dragon.

With that realization, the handsome Prince charged forth, readying his shield and swingling his hammer with all his might. As the handsome Prince attacked, the dragon just whipped its tail. The swat sent the handsome Prince tumbling to a halt, all twisted and tangled.

A Parable

The handsome Prince slowly took the reins of his horse and started to walk dejectedly off in the direction of the woods. The little voice inside of his head kept repeating,

I can't defeat a dragon.
I'm terrified of dragons.
I'll never be able to rescue the beautiful Princess.
I can't defeat a dragon.

The handsome Prince held on to the love he felt for the beautiful Princess and used it to find the courage to continue with his efforts to try to slay the dreaded dragon. He got back up on his horse, gripped his shield and hammer and declared, "I **will** defeat you, Dragon!" After all, he is the handsome Prince: the strongest warrior in all the land!

Lining up again on the pathway leading to the evil Sorcerer's castle, the handsome Prince changed forward as he swung his hammer with all his strength, determined to overpower the scary dragon. But once again, with a blast of fiery breath and an effortless swat of its tail, the dragon sent the handsome Prince tumbling violently to the ground.

As the handsome Prince sat stunned on the ground, the voice inside of his head returned and told him again of his inability to ever defeat a dragon, repeating how he has always been terrified of Dragons and could never defeat such a powerful monster. As he limped away in shame, he noticed the opening to a small cave off to his right. Knowing that he needed to rest his body and regain his strength if he wanted to attempt to defeat the dragon and rescue the beautiful Princess, the handsome Prince decided to take shelter in the cave.

He entered the cave he saw a huge flat rock that looked like it would be a good place for him to rest and try to get his strength back. As he stretched out on the rock to rest,

Encountering a Dragon

the little voice inside his head continued to gain power as it grew louder and louder. The voice reminded him over and over again of his childhood fears: that he is terrified of dragons and he would never be able to defeat a dragon. The handsome Prince started to repeat what the voice was telling him outloud.

Unbeknownst to him, the cave where the handsome Prince had stopped to rest was actually the home of a little Wizard. The little Wizard silently stood in the back of the cave listening to the ongoing moaning and groaning from the handsome Prince. Over and over he moaned,

"I am terrified of Dragons... no matter what I do, I'll never be able to defeat a Dragon... I'll never be able to rescue the beautiful Princess because I can never be as powerful as a dragon... I am a failure."

After some time of the handsome Prince's moaning continuing an overwhelming number of times, the little Wizard decided to come out from the back of the cave where he had been hiding in the shadows. The little Wizard walked up to the handsome Prince, but the prince was too wrapped up in his own sorrows to notice his arrival. So, the little Wizard tapped him on the shoulder and introduced himself as the little Wizard who lives next door to the evil Sorcerer. He explained that he knows all there is to know about the evil Sorcerer and that he had a truth he wanted to share with the handsome Prince. With that, the little Wizard said,

"You have to remember who you are dealing with is an evil Sorcerer and he has put the obstacle in front of you that you fear the most. He probably put obstacles in front of you prior to this that you were able to defeat because of your power and your strength. He does this to give you a sense of power and control. This final obstacle is something that you cannot defeat with your strength and physical

A Parable

power because this obstacle is a creation of your own mind's greatest fear. You continue to believe that dragons are real and to fear that you will never be able to defeat one. As long as you believe this to be true, the evil Sorcerer will use this belief to defeat you."

The little Wizard went on to explain to the handsome Prince that the reality is that the giant, scary dragon doesn't have any real power unless someone engages in battle with it and asked the question, "how many times are you willing to be beat by this dragon?"

With that said, the little Wizard asked the handsome Prince, offered the handsome Prince some final advice:

"When you come upon a force you cannot defeat like the Dragon:
* *Do not try to defeat the Dragon.*
* *Ride forward and face the dragon.*
* *Look the dragon squarely in the eyes.*
* *Put down your hammer and shield.*
* *Do not engage in battle with the dragon*
* *Ride beyond that dragon and rescue the beautiful Princess."*

This advice was unlike any advice that the handsome Prince had ever heard. Minutes turned to hours as the handsome Prince mulled over what the little Wizard had shared. Could it really be true? The handsome Prince had always relied on his physical strength and warrior training to defeat his opponents. It had never occured to him that there was more to being courageous and triumphant than knowing how to fight with weapons. The handsome Prince started pacing back and forth... back and forth... back and forth. He thought about when he was a little boy afraid of dragons. Back then, he had been able to ward off his fear of dragons by reminding himself that the dragons he feared were not real... they were only real if he allowed them to be in his imagination.If this worked for him as a little boy, perhaps the little Wizard was right about this

Encountering a Dragon

same tactic working now. Suddenly, the handsome Prince stopped his pacing. What was he waiting for? The love of his life and his future awaited!

The handsome prince re-mounted his white horse and the took off at a gallop, high and strong towards the entrance of the evil Sorcerer's dark, dungy castle that was guarded by the huge, scary dragon.

The handsome Prince saw the dragon's fiery eyes ready to lash out as he entered through the gate of the dark, dungy castle. Instinctively, he gripped one hand tightly on his shield and the other hand firmly on his mighty hammer; ready to react with force. As he continued to approach, he suddenly heard a little voice in his head. Unlike before, the little voice he heard did not tell him that he would fail. This time, the voice he heard belonged to the little Wizard. He heard the little Wizard's words reminding him that,

> *"The dragon gets its strength from the force that you use in attempting to defeat it. As you approach the dragon, surrender your hammer and shield and face the dragon head-on. Do not attempt to overpower the dragon, as it is a force that can not be defeated. Simply ride beyond the dragon."*

Heeding this wisdom, the handsome Prince bravely continued to advance towards the dragon and the dragon's wings flared, casting a dark shadow across the prince and all of the surrounding land. Fear swept through the handsome Prince and he could feel the temptation to attempt to fight the dragon starting to return. But with resilience, the handsome Prince stopped and looked directly into the eyes of the dragon. Then, with his head held high, the handsome Prince courageously rode beyond the confused dragon.

After encountering the dragon, the handsome Prince

easily found the beautiful Princess and, as promised, he rescued her from the evil Sorcerer's dark, dungy castle with a gallant embrace in his loving arms.

Together, the handsome Prince and the beautiful Princess rode off into the sunset and lived happily ever after in their United Kingdom of Loveland.

THE END

QUESTIONS FOR DISCUSSION

What and how do you relate to each character in the parable?

The Handsome Prince

The Beautiful Princess

The Dragon

Questions for Discussion

The Evil Sorcerer

The Little Wizard

In your own words, describe what you learned about yourself by reading this parable.

Encountering a Dragon

Questions for Discussion

ABOUT THE AUTHORS

    Thurman Strother is the author of *Retired Dragon Fighter* and the co-author of the accompanying parable, *Encountering a Dragon*, which he wrote with his daughter, Alle Byeseda. Working together on both projects brought forth a labor of love, which was fueled by as much laughter as there were tears; both of which guided Thurman's heart and his words. Thurman and Alle refer to this time spent together as, "a reminder of God's presence."

    Thurman is a graduate from the University of Florida. He spent his entire professional life serving the community who helped teach him how to 'dance in the light'. After spending fifteen years with SAFE Recovery Systems in Atlanta, GA, he went on to join the team at Talbott Recovery Campus where he was the Director of Patient Care for fifteen years. In 2010, Thurman joined the team at Foundations Recovery Network where he served as the Clinical Director until his professional reitrement in 2016. Thurman's carrer achievements were acknowledged in 2019 when he received the "Legacy in Treatment Award" from the highly acclaimed Caron Foundation.

    In a perpetual desire to share in the exchange of grace that is so prevalent in the mental health and recovery community, Thurman still supports a weekly After-Care group and volunteers as a regular guest speaker for a group of parents who have lost a child to the disease of addiction.

IF YOU OR SOMEONE YOU LOVE IS SUFFERING FROM MENTAL ILLNESS AND/OR ADDICTION, IT IS NEVER TOO LATE TO **STOP** FIGHTING THOSE DRAGONS!

For more information on seeking help, call 988 from any phone or refer to the resources below.

- **National Association of Mental Illness:** www.nami.org
- **Heather Hayes & Associates**: www.heatherhayes.com

www.ingramcontent.com/pod-product-compliance
Lightning Source LLC
Chambersburg PA
CBHW081257170426
43198CB00017B/2824